toytube takeover

The Ultimate Kid's Guide to YouTube Toy Video Stardom

sarah michaels

ridiculously simple books

Copyright © 2023 by Sarah Michaels

All rights reserved.

No part of this book may be reproduced in any form or by any electronic or mechanical means, including information storage and retrieval systems, without written permission from the author, except for the use of brief quotations in a book review.

contents

Introduction — vii

1. GETTING STARTED: PLANNING YOUR TOY VIDEO — 1
   Unleashing the Idea Storm: Pretend Play Brainstorm Bonanza! — 1
   Toy Casting Call: Picking the Perfect Stars and Props for Your Story! — 3
   Storyboarding 101: Crafting a Master Plan for Your Toy Video Adventure! — 5

2. SETTING THE STAGE: CREATING YOUR FILMING ENVIRONMENT — 9
   Set Design Superstars: DIY Tips for Building Toy Video Wonderlands! — 9
   Lights, Camera, Lumens!: A Guide to Lighting Your Toy Videos Like a Pro! — 11

3. LIGHTS, CAMERA, ACTION! FILMING YOUR TOY VIDEO — 15
   Camera Capers: Filming Your Toy Videos Like a Cinematic Superstar! — 15
   Camera Capers: Filming Your Toy Videos Like a Cinematic Superstar! — 18
   Angle Antics: Capturing Your Toy Tales with Dynamic Camera Moves! — 20
   Sound Bites: Making Your Toy Videos Sing with Crystal Clear Audio! — 22

4. BECOMING A DIRECTOR: GUIDING YOUR TOYS THROUGH THE STORY ... 25

Toyventures: Breathing Life into Your Toys with Movement and Expression! ... 25

Voices Galore: Giving Your Toy Characters Personality with Awesome Voice Acting! ... 27

Toy Movie Magic: Adding Special Effects and Animations for Dazzling Videos! ... 29

5. EDITING YOUR MASTERPIECE: PUTTING IT ALL TOGETHER ... 33

The Magic of Movie-Making: A Kid-Friendly Guide to Video Editing Software! ... 33

Clip-tastic Storytelling: Trimming and Arranging Video Clips Like a Pro! ... 35

Tune-errific Toy Videos: Adding Music, Sound Effects, and Titles for Maximum Fun! ... 38

6. THE FINISHING TOUCHES: POLISHING YOUR VIDEO ... 41

Color-tastic Toy Videos: Color Correction and Filters for a Professional Look! ... 41

Toy Video Troubleshooting: How to Fix Common Audio and Video Issues Like a Pro! ... 43

The Great Export Adventure: Exporting Your Video in the Right Format for YouTube ... 46

7. UPLOADING AND SHARING YOUR
TOY VIDEO ON YOUTUBE — 49
   The YouTube Channel Extravaganza: Creating Your YouTube Account (With a Parental Sidekick) — 49
   The Marvelous World of Titles and Descriptions: Making Your Videos Stand Out — 52
   Crafting the Most Fantabulous Thumbnails: A Guide to Wooing Your Audience — 54

8. BUILDING AN AUDIENCE: PROMOTING YOUR TOY VIDEO CHANNEL — 57
   Spreading the Joy: How to Share Your Masterpiece with Friends and Family — 57
   The Social Media Superhero's Guide to Promoting Videos Responsibly — 59
   The Fantabulous Fusion of YouTuber Friendships — 61

9. STAYING SAFE ONLINE: A GUIDE FOR KIDS AND PARENTS — 65
   The Super-Duper Guide to Staying Safe on YouTube! — 65
   Parental Powers: Unlocking the Secrets of Online Safety! — 67
   The Art of Dodging Cyber-Baddies and Their Mean Messages — 69

Becoming a Pretend Play Toy Video Star: Tips for Success — 71
Conclusion: The Adventure Continues — 77

introduction

the super-duper power of pretend play toy videos!

Once upon a time, in a world full of toys, there were action figures, dolls, and stuffed animals just waiting for someone to bring them to life. But how could they become the stars of their own stories? With the magic of pretend play toy videos, of course! In this section, we'll dive into the awesomeness of pretend play toy videos and why they're both super-duper fun and mind-blowingly educational.

First of all, pretend play toy videos are like a ticket to a land of never-ending adventures. They're like a passport to a world where toys can fly, talk, and even save the day. You can make your toys travel

Introduction

to outer space, battle dragons, or even open their own ice cream shop. The possibilities are as endless as the flavors in a ginormous ice cream sundae!

Now, let's talk about the educational part. Believe it or not, making pretend play toy videos is like a workout for your brain! (But don't worry, you won't need any gym shorts for this kind of workout.) When you create your own toy video stories, you're practicing super-important skills like storytelling, problem-solving, and creativity. Plus, by acting out different characters, you're developing empathy and social skills. Who knew toys could be so smart?

But wait, there's more! Making pretend play toy videos isn't just about flexing your brain muscles; it's also about learning cool technical stuff. You'll learn how to use cameras, lights, and editing software to create videos that look like they were made by a Hollywood pro. By the time you're done, you might just be the next Steven Spielberg or Ava DuVernay of toy videos!

To wrap it all up like a present with a shiny bow, pretend play toy videos are the ultimate combo of fun, adventure, and learning. They're like a superhero with the power to make your toys come alive, teach you new skills, and entertain you all at the same time. So grab your cape (and your favorite toys), because it's time to start your journey as a pretend play toy video creator!

toy videos: the swiss army knife of fun and learning!

Are you ready for some top-secret info? Creating toy videos is like having a Swiss Army knife in your pocket, full of surprises and benefits! Don't worry, we're not talking about real knives here; we're talking about all the amazing things you can gain from making your own toy videos. So, buckle up and let's explore the wonderful world of toy video benefits!

1. Confidence Boost: When you make toy videos, you're the boss, the director, and the star! The more you create, the more you'll believe in yourself and your abilities. Soon, you'll be strutting around like a peacock, knowing you can conquer anything, even a mountain of homework!
2. Friends Galore: Sharing your toy videos with others can help you make new friends who love the same toys and stories as you do. It's like a super-secret club where everyone speaks the same toy language. High-five, fellow toy enthusiasts!

3. Say "Hello" to Patience: Making a toy video might take longer than microwaving a bag of popcorn, but it's totally worth it! With each video, you'll learn the art of patience, which is an essential life skill (especially when you're waiting for your favorite dessert to bake).
4. Super Storytelling Skills: As you create more toy videos, you'll become a master storyteller, spinning tales so epic that even your grandparents will be begging for more! Who knows? You might even write the next best-selling book or hit movie script.
5. Technical Wizardry: Get ready to be the coolest kid on the block as you learn to use cameras, lighting, and editing software like a pro. Soon, you'll be helping your friends and family create their own amazing videos, all thanks to your technical wizardry!
6. Unleash Your Inner Artist: Making toy videos is a fantastic way to express yourself and your ideas. You'll get to try out different styles, themes, and stories, making each video a unique piece of art. Picasso who?

Introduction

As you can see, making toy videos is like having a magical toolbox filled with fun, friends, and fantastic skills. Creating your own toy videos is like opening a treasure chest of awesomeness, ready to make your life more exciting and colorful. So, grab your toys, your camera, and your imagination, and let's dive into the adventure of a lifetime!

youtube: the ultimate canvas for your creative masterpieces!

Imagine a magical place where you can share your wildest ideas, most hilarious jokes, and breathtaking toy adventures with the entire world. Sounds like a dream come true, right? Well, pinch yourself, because this place is real, and it's called YouTube! Let's explore how YouTube can be the ultimate canvas for your colorful creativity and self-expression.

1. The World is Your Stage: With YouTube, you can share your toy videos with people from all corners of the globe. You might become a toy video sensation in Australia, Canada, or even Timbuktu! It's like having your very own world tour, but without the jet lag.

2. Choose Your Own Adventure: On YouTube, you can make videos about anything your heart desires. Love superheroes? Create a series about your action figures saving the day. Mad about cooking? Whip up some play-doh recipes with your favorite chef toys. With YouTube, the sky's the limit!
3. A Community of Creative Geniuses: YouTube is full of other kids just like you, who are passionate about making their own videos. You can learn from them, get inspired, and even collaborate on epic toy adventures. It's like attending a never-ending party with fellow creative geniuses!
4. Show Off Your Unique Style: Your toy videos can be as unique as your fingerprint, showcasing your one-of-a-kind sense of humor, storytelling, and creativity. YouTube is the perfect place to let your inner artist shine and share your voice with the world.
5. Learn and Grow: As you create and share your toy videos on YouTube, you'll learn from feedback, discover new techniques, and improve your skills. It's like having

your very own art school, but without the homework!

So, what are you waiting for? YouTube is like a giant, blank canvas, waiting for you to paint it with your incredible toy video masterpieces. Grab your paintbrush (and your camera), and let's create some unforgettable stories that will dazzle the world!

1 / getting started: planning your toy video

unleashing the idea storm: pretend play brainstorm bonanza!

EVER WONDERED how to catch a tornado of brilliant ideas for your pretend play scenarios? Well, buckle up, because we're about to dive headfirst into a brainstorm bonanza! Here's your top-secret guide to unleashing an idea storm for your toy videos that will blow your socks off (but not literally, because that would be messy).

1. Spy on Your Toys: Take a peek into your toybox and get to know your toys better. What are their superpowers? What are their dreams? What's their favorite ice cream flavor? The more you know, the

more exciting stories you can create with them.

2. Mix and Match Madness: Why not mix up your toys in wild and wacky ways? Maybe your dinosaur wants to be a ballerina, or your action figure dreams of becoming a world-famous chef. The crazier the combination, the more hilarious and unique your stories will be!

3. Time Traveling Tales: Travel through time with your toys, exploring different eras and events. From prehistoric parties to futuristic space adventures, there's no limit to the fun you can have when you let your imagination run wild!

4. Movie Magic: Think of your favorite movies, and imagine how your toys could star in their own version. Would your action figures make a great superhero team? Could your stuffed animals form a rock band? The sky's the limit when it comes to cinematic inspiration!

5. The Power of "What If?": Ask yourself "what if" questions to spark your imagination. What if your toys came to life when no one was looking? What if your dolls had a secret underground lair? The

more "what ifs" you ask, the more fantastic your pretend play scenarios will be!
6. Teamwork Makes the Dream Work: Grab a friend or sibling and brainstorm together. Sometimes, two heads are better than one when it comes to cooking up awesome ideas. Plus, it's double the fun!

Now that you've unleashed the idea storm, it's time to gather those brilliant brainstorm nuggets and create a whirlwind of fantastic pretend play scenarios for your toy videos. So, hold onto your hats (and your toys), and get ready to take the world of YouTube by storm with your imaginative and hilarious toy adventures!

toy casting call: picking the perfect stars and props for your story!

Ready to create a blockbuster toy video? Well, every great movie needs an all-star cast and some snazzy props. So, let's roll out the red carpet and learn how to choose the perfect toys and props to make your story shine brighter than a supernova (but without the space goggles)!

1. The Star-Studded Lineup: Think about which toys would be the best fit for your story. Do you need a brave superhero, a mysterious detective, or a fabulous fashionista? Remember, your toys are the stars of the show, so choose wisely, and don't forget their autographs!
2. The Supporting Cast: Every main character needs some trusty sidekicks. Pick toys that complement your main stars and help bring your story to life. Maybe your robot needs a friendly alien, or your princess could use a loyal pet dragon.
3. All About That Theme: Consider the theme of your story when choosing your toys and props. If you're creating a wild west adventure, cowboy hats and horses might be just the ticket. Planning an epic space battle? Spaceships and laser guns are a must!
4. DIY Props to the Rescue: Can't find the perfect prop for your story? Get creative and make your own! Transform everyday items into amazing props with a little paint, glue, and imagination. A cardboard box can become a treasure chest, and a

plastic cup might turn into a magical goblet!
5. Keep It Simple, Smarty-Pants: While it's tempting to use every toy and prop you own, sometimes less is more. Stick to a few key toys and props that really bring your story to life, and avoid cluttering your video with too many distractions.
6. Safety First: Make sure your toys and props are safe to use and age-appropriate. No need to create a toy video disaster with broken toys or risky props. Save the stunts for the professionals!

With your all-star cast and snazzy props in hand, you're ready to create a toy video that will make Hollywood jealous. So, break out the popcorn, grab your toys, and get ready to create a story that will have your YouTube fans cheering for more!

storyboarding 101: crafting a master plan for your toy video adventure!

Imagine if you could see your whole toy video adventure laid out before your very eyes, like a magical treasure map. Well, grab your pencils and paper, because it's time to learn the ancient art of storyboarding! (Okay, it's not really ancient, but it's still pretty cool.) Let's dive into the wonderful world of crafting a simple storyboard for your video.

1. The Big Picture: Start by jotting down the main events of your story. Think of these as the key stops on your toy video adventure. Will your action figure save the day? Will your stuffed animals throw a surprise party? Write down your brilliant ideas, and watch your story come to life!
2. Frame by Frame: Now, break your story into smaller scenes, like a comic book. Draw a series of boxes (or "frames") on a piece of paper, and sketch out the action for each scene. No need to be the next Michelangelo; stick figures will do just fine!
3. Lights, Camera, Dialogue!: Add speech bubbles or captions to your frames to show what your toys are saying or thinking. This will help you keep track of your story's dialogue and make sure your toys' conversations are as snappy and hilarious as a comedy show.
4. A Picture is Worth a Thousand Words: Use arrows, symbols, or doodles to show movement and camera angles in your

storyboard. This will help you plan out your shots and make sure your toy video is as exciting and dynamic as a roller coaster ride!

5. Color Your World: If you're feeling extra artsy, add some color to your storyboard to bring your scenes to life. This can help you visualize your story better and make your storyboard as vibrant as a rainbow!
6. Keep it Flexible: Remember, your storyboard is a tool to help you plan your video, but it's not set in stone. Feel free to change things up or improvise as you film. After all, the best stories have a little bit of surprise and spontaneity!

With your trusty storyboard in hand, you'll be ready to tackle your toy video adventure like a pro. So, sharpen those pencils, gather your toys, and let's set sail on an epic journey through the magical land of storyboarding!

2 / setting the stage: creating your filming environment

set design superstars: diy tips for building toy video wonderlands!

READY TO TRANSFORM your toy videos into cinematic masterpieces? It's time to put on your hard hat and become a set design superstar! With a pinch of creativity and a dash of elbow grease, you'll be crafting toy video wonderlands that'll make your viewers say, "WOW!"

1. Cardboard Kingdoms: Save those old cardboard boxes from the recycling bin, because they're about to become your new best friends! Cut, fold, and paint your way to amazing sets, from majestic castles to futuristic space stations.

2. The Power of Paper: Construction paper, poster board, and even old magazines can be your secret weapons for creating colorful backgrounds and eye-catching props. Snip, glue, and collage your way to set design stardom!
3. Repurpose and Reuse: Take a look around your house for items that can be transformed into fantastic sets and props. An empty egg carton could become a cozy bed for your toy animals, while a shoebox might make the perfect stage for your action figures.
4. Fabric Fun: Old sheets, blankets, and towels can be used to create interesting backgrounds and textures for your sets. Drape them, fold them, or even cut them up to create a whole new world for your toys to explore.
5. LEGO Landscapes: If you have a collection of LEGOs or building blocks, use them to construct epic cities, towering mountains, or even a deep-sea adventure for your toys. Bonus points for using mismatched colors to create a wacky, one-of-a-kind set!
6. Nature's Palette: Bring the great outdoors to your toy videos with natural materials

like leaves, sticks, and rocks. Create a lush jungle for your toy animals, or build a rustic log cabin for your dolls. Mother Nature would be proud!
7. Lights, Camera, Action Figures!: Don't forget to add some pizzazz to your sets with fun action figures, dolls, and toy accessories. The more unique and eye-catching your props, the more your toy video will stand out from the crowd.

So, roll up your sleeves, grab your craft supplies, and let's get ready to build some jaw-dropping toy video wonderlands that'll leave your viewers speechless (in a good way, of course)! And who knows? You might just inspire the next generation of set design superstars!

lights, camera, lumens!: a guide to lighting your toy videos like a pro!

Are you ready to illuminate your toy videos with the power of a thousand suns? (Okay, maybe not that bright.) Grab your flashlights, lamps, and glittery disco balls, because it's time to learn how to use lighting to enhance your video's look and make your toys shine like the superstars they are!

1. Natural Wonders: The sun is your best friend when it comes to lighting your videos. Film near a window or outside to take advantage of that big, bright ball of light in the sky. Just remember to wear sunscreen on your outdoor adventures!
2. Let There Be Lamps: If you're filming indoors or in a dimly lit space, lamps are here to save the day! Experiment with different types of lamps and bulbs to create the perfect mood for your toy video. Soft, warm light for a cozy scene? Check! Bright, cool light for an action-packed adventure? You got it!
3. Flashlight Frenzy: Handheld flashlights are like magic wands that can instantly transform your video's look. Use them to create dramatic shadows, spooky effects, or even a toy disco dance party. (Cue the funky music!)
4. Tinfoil Tricks: Line a cardboard box with tinfoil to create a DIY light reflector. This nifty contraption will bounce light onto your toys and make them look as radiant as a unicorn bathed in moonlight.
5. Color Me Impressed: Add a splash of color to your video by covering your light

sources with colored cellophane or tissue paper. This simple trick can turn your toy video into a dazzling light show or set the mood for a mysterious adventure. Just be sure not to let the paper touch hot light bulbs!
6. Shadows and Silhouettes: Play with shadows and silhouettes to add depth and drama to your video. Position your lights at different angles to create interesting shapes and patterns. Your toys will look like they're starring in their very own film noir masterpiece!
7. Trial and Error: There's no one-size-fits-all solution for lighting your toy videos. Experiment with different light sources, angles, and colors to find the perfect combination for your story. Remember, practice makes perfect, and sometimes the best ideas come from happy accidents!

With these illuminating tips, your toy videos will be glowing with awesomeness, and your audience will be left starry-eyed in wonder. So, light up your imagination and get ready to create toy video magic that'll leave your viewers begging for an encore!

3 / lights, camera, action! filming your toy video

camera capers: filming your toy videos like a cinematic superstar!

LIGHTS? Check! Toys? Check! Glorious sets and backgrounds? Double check! Now, it's time to unleash your inner Spielberg and learn some basic camera techniques to turn your toy videos into box-office hits! (Well, at least YouTube hits.) Ready, set, action!

1. Steady as She Goes: No one likes a shaky video that makes them feel like they're riding a roller coaster. Use a tripod, a stack of books, or even your own steady hands to keep your camera stable and your audience free from motion sickness.

2. Zoom Zoom Zoom: Get up close and personal with your toys by using your camera's zoom feature or by simply moving the camera closer. This will help your viewers feel like they're part of the action and make your toys look larger than life!
3. Lights, Camera, Angles!: Experiment with different camera angles to add excitement and variety to your video. Film from above for a bird's-eye view, from below for a dramatic, larger-than-life perspective, or from the side for a classic shot. The sky's the limit!
4. The Power of Panning: Slowly move your camera from side to side to capture a wide, sweeping shot of your epic toy landscape. This technique, called panning, can make your video feel like it's part of a big-budget Hollywood production!
5. Fade In, Fade Out: Learn how to use your camera's built-in effects, like fading in or out, to create smooth transitions between scenes. These nifty tricks will give your toy video a polished, professional feel, and make you look like a seasoned filmmaker!

6. Focus on the Fun: Keep your toys in focus by using your camera's autofocus feature or by manually adjusting the focus ring. Blurry toys are sad toys, so make sure your video stars are sharp and ready for their close-ups!
7. The Rule of Thirds: Divide your screen into nine equal sections using imaginary lines, like a tic-tac-toe board. Place your toys and props along these lines or at their intersections for a balanced, visually appealing composition. Trust us, your viewers will thank you!
8. Take Your Time: Be patient when filming your toy videos. Take the time to set up your shots, adjust your camera settings, and practice your camera moves. Remember, Rome wasn't built in a day, and neither are award-winning toy videos!

With these camera capers in your filmmaking toolbox, you'll be ready to capture your toy's adventures like a true cinematic superstar! So, grab your camera, channel your inner director, and let's make some toy video magic that'll leave your audience shouting, "Bravo!"

Sarah Michaels

camera capers: filming your toy videos like a cinematic superstar!

Lights? Check! Toys? Check! Glorious sets and backgrounds? Double check! Now, it's time to unleash your inner Spielberg and learn some basic camera techniques to turn your toy videos into box-office hits! (Well, at least YouTube hits.) Ready, set, action!

1. Steady as She Goes: No one likes a shaky video that makes them feel like they're riding a roller coaster. Use a tripod, a stack of books, or even your own steady hands to keep your camera stable and your audience free from motion sickness.
2. Zoom Zoom Zoom: Get up close and personal with your toys by using your camera's zoom feature or by simply moving the camera closer. This will help your viewers feel like they're part of the action and make your toys look larger than life!
3. Lights, Camera, Angles!: Experiment with different camera angles to add excitement and variety to your video. Film from above for a bird's-eye view, from below for a dramatic, larger-than-life perspective, or

from the side for a classic shot. The sky's the limit!
4. The Power of Panning: Slowly move your camera from side to side to capture a wide, sweeping shot of your epic toy landscape. This technique, called panning, can make your video feel like it's part of a big-budget Hollywood production!
5. Fade In, Fade Out: Learn how to use your camera's built-in effects, like fading in or out, to create smooth transitions between scenes. These nifty tricks will give your toy video a polished, professional feel, and make you look like a seasoned filmmaker!
6. Focus on the Fun: Keep your toys in focus by using your camera's autofocus feature or by manually adjusting the focus ring. Blurry toys are sad toys, so make sure your video stars are sharp and ready for their close-ups!
7. The Rule of Thirds: Divide your screen into nine equal sections using imaginary lines, like a tic-tac-toe board. Place your toys and props along these lines or at their intersections for a balanced, visually appealing composition. Trust us, your viewers will thank you!

8. Take Your Time: Be patient when filming your toy videos. Take the time to set up your shots, adjust your camera settings, and practice your camera moves. Remember, Rome wasn't built in a day, and neither are award-winning toy videos!

With these camera capers in your filmmaking toolbox, you'll be ready to capture your toy's adventures like a true cinematic superstar! So, grab your camera, channel your inner director, and let's make some toy video magic that'll leave your audience shouting, "Bravo!"

angle antics: capturing your toy tales with dynamic camera moves!

Grab your director's chair and put on your thinking cap, because it's time to explore the wacky world of camera angles for dynamic storytelling! With a few clever camera moves, you can turn your toy video into a visual feast that'll have your viewers on the edge of their seats. Let's dive in!

1. High and Mighty: A high-angle shot, taken from above your toys, can make them look small and vulnerable. This is perfect for a

scene where your toys need to overcome a big challenge or face a giant (gasp!) antagonist.

2. Low and Bold: On the flip side, a low-angle shot, taken from below your toys, can make them look powerful and larger than life. Use this angle when your toys are feeling super confident or about to save the day!

3. Eye Spy: Capture the action from your toy's point of view by placing the camera at their eye level. This immersive angle will make your viewers feel like they're right there in the thick of the adventure, battling dragons or solving mysteries alongside your toys.

4. Over-the-Shoulder Shenanigans: To show a conversation between two toys, try an over-the-shoulder shot. Position the camera behind one toy, so their shoulder is in the foreground, while the other toy is in the background. This classic angle will make your viewers feel like they're part of the action, listening in on top-secret toy gossip!

5. Tilt-a-Whirl: Add some drama to your video by tilting the camera up or down

while filming. This technique, called a Dutch angle, can create a sense of disorientation or tension in your story. Use it sparingly, though, or your viewers might get a case of the dizzies!
6. The Great Outdoors: If your toy story takes place outside, try using natural features like trees, hills, or even puddles to create interesting camera angles. Capture your toys' adventures from the top of a tree or the bottom of a hill for some truly epic shots.

Now that you're an expert in angle antics, your toy videos will be bursting with dynamic storytelling that keeps your audience glued to the screen! So, grab your camera, gather your toys, and let's create cinematic masterpieces that'll have your viewers shouting, "Encore!"

sound bites: making your toy videos sing with crystal clear audio!

Move over, silent films, because it's time to crank up the volume and learn how to record clear audio for your toy videos! With a little know-how, you can capture the sweet sounds of your toy adventures and make your audience feel like they're right there with you. Ready to make some noise? Let's go!

1. Whispering Wind: Film indoors or in a quiet spot outside to avoid capturing unwanted background noise, like chatty squirrels or cars honking in the distance. Your toys deserve their moment in the spotlight, without any distractions!
2. Mic Check 1, 2: If your camera has a built-in microphone, make sure it's not covered by your hands or any pesky props. You want your toy's voices to be loud and clear, not muffled and mysterious!
3. The Power of the Smartphone: If your camera's built-in microphone isn't cutting it, try using your smartphone to record audio. Just remember to sync the audio and video later, so your toys don't end up looking like they're in a badly dubbed movie!
4. Pop Star Dreams: Consider investing in a budget-friendly external microphone, like a lavalier or shotgun mic, for better audio quality. Your toys will sound like they're ready to hit the big stage or star in their own blockbuster!

5. Quiet on the Set!: While filming, try to minimize any background noise, like barking dogs, noisy siblings, or the hum of the refrigerator. You don't want your toy's epic battle scene to be upstaged by a rumbling tummy!
6. Sound Effects Extravaganza: Use free sound effect libraries or make your own sounds to add extra pizzazz to your video. The sound of clashing swords, roaring engines, or even a well-timed "boing!" can make your toy story even more entertaining!

With these sound bites in your audio toolbox, your toy videos will be music to your audience's ears! So, grab your microphone, quiet your surroundings, and let's create toy adventures that sound as amazing as they look! Your viewers will be shouting, "Hooray for clear audio!"

4 /
becoming a director: guiding your toys through the story

toyventures: breathing life into your toys with movement and expression!

LIGHTS, camera, action! Now that you've got the technical side of toy videos covered, it's time to turn your toys into Oscar-worthy actors with expressive movements and captivating performances. So, let's dive into the magical world of toyventures and learn how to make your toys come alive on screen!

1. Puppetry Prowess: Use your hands, strings, or sticks to move your toys around, making them walk, run, jump, or dance. Remember, practice makes perfect, and soon you'll be a master puppeteer!

2. Emoting Emojis: To help your toys show their emotions, use stickers, clay, or tiny props to create different facial expressions. You can even use simple cutouts of eyebrows, mouths, and other features to switch up their emotions as the story unfolds!
3. The Power of Poses: Strike a pose! Arrange your toys in dynamic positions to express their emotions or actions. A superhero landing or a dramatic arm gesture can speak volumes!
4. Slow-Mo Mojo: Use slow-motion effects or film in slow motion to add drama and suspense to your video. Your toys will look like they're starring in their own action-packed blockbuster!
5. Fast and Furious: On the flip side, use fast-motion effects or time-lapse to speed up your toy's movements for comedic effect or to show the passage of time. Your toys will be zipping around like roadrunners!
6. The Sound of Silence: Don't be afraid to use moments of stillness and silence to build tension or emphasize a dramatic scene. Sometimes, less is more when it comes to making your toys come alive!

7. Toy Talk: Use different voices or enlist the help of friends and family to give your toys their own unique personalities. With a little voice acting magic, your toys will be the talk of the town!

With these toyventures tips, your toys will come to life on screen with movement and expression that captivates your audience. So, roll out the red carpet and let your toys take center stage, ready to steal the hearts of viewers everywhere! They'll be shouting, "Give those toys an Oscar!"

voices galore: giving your toy characters personality with awesome voice acting!

Time to warm up those vocal cords, because we're about to dive into the wonderful world of voice acting! With a few nifty tricks, you can bring your toy characters to life and make them sound like they stepped right out of a Hollywood blockbuster. Let's get those toy voices talking!

1. Play with Pitch: Experiment with high and low pitches to create unique voices for your toys. A squeaky voice might be

perfect for a tiny mouse, while a deep, booming voice could suit a mighty superhero!

2. Pacing and Pauses: Change the speed of your speech to add variety to your toy's dialogue. A fast-talking character might be super excited, while a slow, deliberate speaker might be wise and thoughtful.
3. Accents and Dialects: Try out different accents and dialects to give your toys a distinct sound. You can even mix and match accents to create a totally unique voice that'll make your toy stand out from the crowd!
4. Emotional Rollercoaster: Show your toy's emotions through your voice acting. A happy toy might sound cheery and upbeat, while a sad toy might have a softer, more somber tone.
5. Mannerisms and Catchphrases: Add in fun mannerisms or catchphrases to make your toy's voice even more memorable. Just imagine a toy pirate who says "Arr matey!" or a toy robot that repeats "Beep boop"!
6. Sound Effects and Noises: Don't be afraid to get creative with sound effects and noises. From animal sounds to funny

grunts and laughs, these extra touches can make your toy's voice truly one-of-a-kind!
7. Practice Makes Perfect: The more you practice, the better your voice acting will become. Try recording yourself and listening back to improve your performance. You'll be a voice acting superstar in no time!

With these voice acting tips, your toy characters will come to life with unique voices that captivate and entertain your audience. So, take a deep breath, and let's turn your toy adventures into a symphony of voices that'll leave your viewers cheering for an encore!

toy movie magic: adding special effects and animations for dazzling videos!

You've mastered the art of filming and editing, but now it's time to sprinkle some extra sparkle onto your toy videos with special effects and animations! Get ready to unleash your inner movie magician and transform your toy adventures into dazzling spectacles that'll leave your audience spellbound!

1. Animation Sensation: Use stop-motion animation to bring your toys to life in a whole new way. With just a camera and some patience, you can create epic toy adventures frame by frame. Get ready for your toys to become stop-motion stars!
2. Green Screen Dreams: Want to transport your toys to the moon or the bottom of the ocean? A green screen can make it happen! With some green fabric or paper and a little video editing magic, you can create amazing backgrounds and settings for your toy videos.
3. Sparkling Filters: Add a touch of glitz and glamour to your video with fun filters and effects. From sparkles and rainbows to vintage film styles, there's a whole world of filters waiting to jazz up your toy adventures!
4. Explosive Action: Use special effects like fake explosions, laser beams, or smoke to make your toy videos action-packed and thrilling. Just remember not to go overboard – you don't want to turn your video into a special effects extravaganza that steals the spotlight from your toys!

5. Text-tastic Animations: Make your titles and captions come to life with animated text effects. From bouncing letters to swirling words, these text-tastic animations will add a splash of fun to your video.
6. Silly Stickers: Add funny stickers, emojis, or doodles to your video for a playful touch. Your toys will love having their own virtual props and accessories!
7. Layering it Up: Combine special effects, animations, and other elements in layers to create a rich, immersive toy video experience. With a little practice, you'll be a layering pro in no time!

With these special effects and animation tips, your toy videos will become magical, mesmerizing masterpieces that leave your audience spellbound. So, put on your movie magician's hat and let's make some toy movie magic that'll have your viewers shouting, "Encore, encore!"

5 / editing your masterpiece: putting it all together

the magic of movie-making: a kid-friendly guide to video editing software!

LIGHTS, camera...wait, what about the editing? Filming your toy adventures is just the beginning, because now it's time to transform your raw footage into a dazzling masterpiece with the help of some magical video editing software. Don't worry, it's not as scary as it sounds! Let's dive into the wonderful world of movie-making for kids!

1. Editing Elves: Start by choosing a kid-friendly video editing software. There are plenty of free options available, like iMovie, Windows Movie Maker, or even

mobile apps like KineMaster and Adobe Premiere Rush. These editing elves will help you make your toy videos shine!
2. The Cutting Room Floor: Once you've picked your software, import your video clips and start cutting and trimming your footage. Remember, practice makes perfect, so don't be afraid to make mistakes as you learn to slice and dice your way to a seamless video.
3. Snazzy Transitions: Add cool transitions between scenes to give your video a professional touch. From classic fades to playful wipes, there's a whole world of snazzy transitions waiting for you to explore!
4. Sounds Like Fun: Don't forget to add your recorded audio, music, and sound effects to your video. With a few well-timed sound bites, your toy video will sound as awesome as it looks!
5. Text-tacular Titles: Use your video editing software to add fun titles, captions, and credits to your video. Choose playful fonts and colors to make your text-tacular titles pop!

6. Special Effects Extravaganza: Unleash your inner movie magician with special effects like slow motion, fast motion, or even green screen magic. The sky's the limit when it comes to creating spellbinding toy adventures!
7. Save and Share: Once your video is polished and perfect, save your masterpiece and share it with the world! Get ready for your toys to become the next big stars of YouTube!

With these magical movie-making tips, you'll be well on your way to becoming a video editing wizard. So, grab your editing wand and let's turn your toy footage into a cinematic sensation that'll have your audience shouting, "Hooray for Hollywood!"

clip-tastic storytelling: trimming and arranging video clips like a pro!

So, you've got a mountain of video clips, and now it's time to trim and arrange them into a riveting tale of toy adventure! Fear not, future film director, because we're here to guide you through the clip-tastic world of storytelling with your video clips. Let's get those scissors snipping and that story flowing!

1. The Mighty Trim: Start by watching your video clips and deciding which parts you want to keep and which parts need the snip-snip treatment. Remember, it's all about keeping the best bits and ditching the rest to create a tight, captivating story.
2. Puzzle Pieces: Think of your video clips like puzzle pieces that need to be arranged in the right order to create a complete picture. Experiment with different clip arrangements to find the perfect storytelling flow.
3. Smooth Transitions: Make sure your video clips flow seamlessly from one to the next by using smooth transitions. Try fading, dissolving, or even some funky wipes to keep your audience engaged and entertained.
4. Pacing is Key: Pay attention to the pacing of your story. Mix fast-paced action scenes with slower, more emotional moments to keep your viewers hooked from start to finish.

5. Less is More: Sometimes, less is more when it comes to storytelling. Don't be afraid to cut out unnecessary scenes or dialogue to keep your story focused and your audience engaged.
6. Sound and Vision: Don't forget to consider how your audio, music, and sound effects work with your video clips. Use sound to enhance the mood and atmosphere of your story, and make sure it syncs up perfectly with your visuals.
7. Finishing Touches: Once you've arranged your video clips and perfected your story, add titles, captions, and credits to complete your masterpiece. Don't forget to save your work and share it with the world!

With these clip-tastic storytelling tips, you'll be trimming and arranging video clips like a pro in no time. So, grab those virtual scissors and let's create a toy adventure that'll have your viewers on the edge of their seats, begging for more!

tune-errific toy videos: adding music, sound effects, and titles for maximum fun!

Ready to take your toy video from good to tune-errific? Adding music, sound effects, and titles is like putting the cherry on top of a scrumptious ice cream sundae. So, let's get ready to sprinkle some musical magic onto your toy adventure and turn your video into a symphony of fun!

1. Musical Masterpieces: Choose the perfect background music to set the mood for your toy adventure. From action-packed tunes to gentle melodies, the right music can make your video come alive. Just make sure to pick royalty-free music or create your own to avoid any copyright issues.
2. Sound Effect Extravaganza: Amplify the fun with wacky sound effects! From toy car revs to superhero swooshes, the right sound effects can add a whole new dimension to your video. Explore free sound effect libraries or even record your own!
3. Sync it Up: Make sure your music and sound effects sync perfectly with your

video clips. It's like a dance – everything needs to be in harmony to create a magical movie experience.
4. Title Time: Create fun and eye-catching titles for your video. Use playful fonts and colors to make your titles stand out, and don't be afraid to get creative with animations and effects.
5. Caption Capers: Add captions to your video to help tell your story and make it accessible to all viewers. Use easy-to-read fonts and colors, and remember to keep it short and sweet.
6. Credit Where Credit's Due: Don't forget to add credits at the end of your video to give a shout-out to all the amazing people (and toys) who helped make your video a reality. You can even add a blooper reel or a teaser for your next video!
7. Preview Party: Before you export your finished video, watch it all the way through to make sure everything looks and sounds perfect. If you spot any mistakes or need to make changes, now's the time to do it!

With these tune-errific tips, your toy videos will

be brimming with music, sound effects, and titles that'll make your audience want to sing and dance along. So, let's hit the high notes and create a toy video masterpiece that'll have viewers shouting, "Encore, encore!"

6 / the finishing touches: polishing your video

color-tastic toy videos: color correction and filters for a professional look!

READY TO MAKE your toy videos look like they were made by a Hollywood director? It's time to dive into the colorful world of color correction and filters! With a few magical tweaks, your video will go from ordinary to color-tastic in no time. So, let's get ready to paint the screen with vibrant hues and create a toy video that's truly a feast for the eyes!

1. What's the Hue: First things first, let's talk about hue. Hue is the shade or tint of a color. Make sure the colors in your video are accurate and true to life. If something

looks off, like your red toy car looks a bit too orange, adjust the hue to make it picture-perfect.
2. Brighten Up: Make your video shine by adjusting the brightness. If your video is too dark or too bright, it can be hard to see all the fantastic toy action. So, find that sweet spot where everything is crystal clear and full of life.
3. Contrast Control: Contrast is the difference between the darkest and lightest parts of your video. Adjust the contrast to make your toy characters really stand out from the background and add depth to your video.
4. Saturation Sensation: Saturation is how intense or dull the colors in your video appear. Play around with the saturation to make your colors really pop, but be careful not to go overboard – you don't want your toys to look like they've been dipped in neon paint!
5. Fun with Filters: Filters are like magical overlays that can change the look and feel of your video in an instant. Try out different filters to create cool effects, like a vintage toy commercial or a futuristic

toy adventure. The possibilities are endless!
6. Consistency is Key: Make sure the color correction and filters you use are consistent throughout your video. You want your viewers to feel like they're watching a cohesive story, not a patchwork quilt of mismatched colors and effects.
7. Practice Makes Perfect: Experiment with different color correction and filter settings until you find the perfect look for your toy video. Remember, practice makes perfect, and soon you'll be a color-tastic video wizard!

With these color correction and filter tips, your toy videos will look like they were made by a true pro. So, grab your color wheel and let's create a visual masterpiece that'll have viewers oohing and aahing over your color-tastic creations!

toy video troubleshooting: how to fix common audio and video issues like a pro!

Uh-oh! Did your toy video hit a bump in the road? Don't worry! Every great director faces a few challenges along the way. With these super-duper troubleshooting tips, you'll be able to fix common audio and video issues and get your toy video back on track in no time. So, let's put on our detective hats and solve these toy video mysteries together!

1. Muffled Audio Mayhem: Is your audio sounding like your toys are talking into a pillow? Try moving your microphone closer to your toy characters, adjusting the audio levels, or using a pop filter to clear up any muffled sounds.
2. Echo Extravaganza: Do your toy characters sound like they're in a spooky cave with lots of echoes? You can fix this by using blankets or pillows to absorb the sound, changing your recording location, or applying noise reduction in your editing software.
3. Shaky Video Shenanigans: Does your video look like it was filmed during an earthquake? To fix this, use a tripod or a steady surface to hold your camera still. You can also try using your editing software's stabilization feature to smooth out any shaky footage.

4. Blurry Video Blues: Are your toy characters looking a little fuzzy? Make sure your camera lens is clean and that you're filming in good lighting. Also, check your camera's focus settings to ensure your toys are always in sharp detail.
5. Chopping and Popping Audio: Is your audio full of annoying clicks and pops? This might be due to a poor connection or interference. Check your cables, try a different microphone, or use your editing software to remove any unwanted noises.
6. Synchronization Slip-ups: Are your toy characters' mouths moving, but the words aren't matching up? Adjust the timing of your audio and video clips in your editing software to make sure everything is perfectly in sync.
7. Lost in Transition: Are your video transitions looking a bit jumpy or out of place? Double-check your editing timeline to make sure your clips are properly aligned and that your transitions are smooth and seamless.

With these troubleshooting tips in your toy video toolkit, you'll be able to conquer any audio or video hiccup that comes your way. So, let's put on our superhero capes and save the day by fixing those common issues like the toy video pros we are! Onward to toy video greatness!

the great export adventure: exporting your video in the right format for youtube

Congratulations, young director! You've filmed, edited, and polished your toy video masterpiece. Now, it's time to take the next big step on our toy video journey: exporting your video in the perfect format for YouTube! But fear not, for we have the ultimate guide to help you navigate the great export adventure. So, put on your explorer hat, and let's dive into the wild world of video formats!

1. The Magic of MP4: The first thing you need to know is that YouTube's favorite video format is MP4. It's like the peanut butter to YouTube's jelly. So when you're ready to export your video, make sure you select the MP4 format for a perfect pairing!
2. Resolution Riddles: Next up, let's talk about resolution. YouTube loves high-quality videos, so you'll want to choose a

resolution that makes your toy video shine! For most devices, 1080p (1920x1080) is the sweet spot. But if you've filmed your video in 4K, go ahead and show off those extra pixels!

3. Frame Rate Fun: Frame rate is the number of frames your video shows per second. The higher the frame rate, the smoother your video will look. Most videos on YouTube use a frame rate of 30 frames per second (fps), but you can also use 24 fps or 60 fps if you're feeling fancy.
4. Bitrate Bonanza: Bitrate is all about how much data your video uses. A higher bitrate means better quality but a larger file size. For most toy videos, a bitrate of around 8-12 Mbps should be more than enough to make your video look great without taking up too much space.
5. Audio Awesome-ness: Don't forget about your audio! YouTube recommends using the AAC audio codec with a bitrate of 128 kbps or higher. This will ensure your toy characters' voices are crystal clear and ready to impress your viewers.
6. Export Settings Extravaganza: Most video editing software has presets for exporting

videos to YouTube. Look for a setting called "YouTube" or "Web" to make sure your video has the right settings for a smooth upload.
7. Patience, Young Grasshopper: Exporting your video can take a while, especially if you're working with a high-resolution file. So, be patient and maybe grab a snack while you wait for your video to be transformed into a YouTube-ready masterpiece.

And there you have it, brave explorer! With these tips, you'll conquer the great export adventure and send your toy video off into the wild world of YouTube. So, get ready to sit back, relax, and watch your toy video dazzle viewers with its perfect format and outstanding quality! Hip-hip-hooray for the great export adventure!

7 /
uploading and sharing your toy video on youtube

the youtube channel extravaganza: creating your youtube account (with a parental sidekick)

LADIES AND GENTLEMEN, boys and girls, the moment you've been waiting for has arrived! It's time to create your very own YouTube account and channel. But wait! Before you jump into the internet ocean, make sure you have your parental sidekick by your side. So, grab Mom, Dad, or another trusty grown-up, and let's embark on this fantastic YouTube journey together.

1. The Dynamic Duo: First things first, make sure you're working as a team with your parental sidekick. Remember, you must be

at least 13 years old to create a YouTube account, so your grown-up will be the one signing up on your behalf.

2. The Great Google Account: To create a YouTube channel, you'll need a Google Account. If your parental sidekick doesn't have one, head over to accounts.google.com and sign up for a new account. If they already have one, give them a high-five and move on to the next step!

3. The YouTube Channel Expedition: With your grown-up's Google Account ready, visit youtube.com and click on "Sign In" in the top-right corner. Enter the Google Account email and password, then click on your profile icon in the top-right corner again. Now, select "Create a channel" from the dropdown menu.

4. The Channel Name Quest: Time to choose a fantastic name for your channel! This name will represent you and your awesome toy videos. Make it fun, catchy, and unforgettable. Once you've decided, type it in and click "Create."

5. The Profile Picture Parade: Next, you'll need a profile picture for your channel.

Choose an image that represents your channel's theme or your toy characters. Make it colorful and eye-catching to attract viewers. Remember, your parental sidekick should help you with this step too!

6. The Channel Art Adventure: The channel art is like a billboard for your channel. Create an exciting banner that showcases the fun and excitement of your toy videos. You can use a photo, a drawing, or even some cool text. Just make sure it's family-friendly and follows YouTube's guidelines.

7. The Channel Description Delight: In the "About" tab, write a brief and entertaining description of your channel. Explain what your toy videos are about and what viewers can expect. Be creative, and let your personality shine!

8. The Parental Sidekick Stamp of Approval: Make sure your parental sidekick reviews and approves everything before you hit "Save" and "Publish." They'll be your trusty guide in making sure everything is in tip-top shape.

Voila! You've now created your very own YouTube channel with the help of your parental sidekick. It's time to start uploading your fantastic toy videos and sharing them with the world. So, prepare yourself for the magical YouTube journey, and don't forget to give your parental sidekick a big thank-you for their help! The YouTube universe awaits your toy video greatness!

the marvelous world of titles and descriptions: making your videos stand out

Hold onto your hats, aspiring YouTubers! It's time to dive into the fantastical realm of titles and descriptions. After all, you've spent hours creating your toy masterpiece, so why not give it the perfect title and description to make it truly shine? With a little dash of wit, a pinch of humor, and a sprinkle of imagination, you'll be whipping up show-stopping titles and descriptions in no time.

1. The Terrific Title: Think of your video title as the flashy, neon sign that invites viewers to enter the magical world of your toy video. It should be short, catchy, and downright irresistible. Try to include keywords related to your video's content,

like the toy's name or the theme of your pretend play.
2. The Dazzling Description: Your video description is like a secret treasure map, guiding viewers through the enchanting land of your toy video. Start with a brief but exciting summary of what happens in the video. Make sure to include those all-important keywords and maybe even a fun joke or two.
3. The Magnificent Keywords: In both your title and description, you'll want to include keywords that help viewers find your video. These keywords are like secret codes that YouTube uses to match your video with people who want to watch it. So, choose words and phrases that are relevant to your video's content and use them wisely.
4. The Enchanting Emojis: Emojis can be a fun way to add a little extra pizzazz to your title and description. But remember, too much of a good thing can be overwhelming. So, use emojis sparingly and only when they truly add to the magic of your title and description.

5. The Captivating Call-to-Action: To wrap up your dazzling description, include a call-to-action that encourages viewers to like, share, and subscribe to your channel. After all, every great toy adventure deserves an adoring audience!

With your marvelous title and description in place, your toy video is ready to take the YouTube world by storm. But remember, young YouTubers, with great power comes great responsibility. So, use your title and description powers wisely, and you'll soon be the talk of the toy town! And when your video gains fame and adoration, don't forget to thank the wondrous world of titles and descriptions for helping your video become a true sensation.

crafting the most fantabulous thumbnails: a guide to wooing your audience

Attention, future YouTube stars! Are you ready to make your videos sparkle and shine like the brightest stars in the sky? It's time to learn the secret art of creating custom thumbnails that will leave viewers absolutely spellbound. Let's embark on a journey to create the most fantabulous, eye-catching, and irresistible thumbnails YouTube has ever seen!

1. The Importance of Thumbnails: In the magical world of YouTube, thumbnails are like little doorways to your video's universe. If they're enticing, intriguing, and oh-so-fabulous, people will be drawn to click and watch your video. So, let's get those creative juices flowing and make your thumbnail a masterpiece!
2. The Perfect Picture: First, you'll need a captivating image that represents the essence of your video. You can use a screenshot from the video, a photo you took yourself, or a combination of both. Just make sure it's clear, high-quality, and showcases the excitement of your toy video.
3. The Wonderful World of Text: Adding text to your thumbnail can help explain your video's content and make it stand out. Choose a short, snappy phrase that sums up your video and use a bold, easy-to-read font. Remember, sometimes less is more, so don't cram too many words onto your thumbnail.

4. The Power of Colors: Use bright, contrasting colors to make your thumbnail pop! Think about how superheroes wear colorful costumes to stand out from the crowd – your thumbnail should do the same. Choose colors that complement your image and text, and you'll have a thumbnail that's truly marvelous.
5. The Finishing Touches: To put the cherry on top of your fantastic thumbnail, consider adding a border or some fun shapes to frame your image. Just be careful not to go overboard – you want your thumbnail to be eye-catching, not cluttered.

Once you've crafted your fantabulous custom thumbnail, your video will be ready to enchant viewers far and wide. With your captivating video, marvelous title, dazzling description, and now your irresistible thumbnail, you'll be well on your way to YouTube stardom. And as you watch the views roll in, remember to take a moment to appreciate the magical power of the perfect thumbnail – after all, it's the tiny detail that makes a world of difference!

8 / building an audience: promoting your toy video channel

spreading the joy: how to share your masterpiece with friends and family

BEHOLD, young YouTubers! You've created a masterpiece of a video, sprinkled with wit, humor, and a dash of toy-tastic magic. Now it's time to share your creation with the world – or at least with your friends, family, and possibly your adorable pet hamster, Mr. Fluffernutter. Here's a guide to spreading joy and laughter with your video, one share at a time.

1. The Art of Email: It may seem like a relic from the ancient days of the internet, but email is still an excellent way to share your

video. Just copy the link to your video, paste it into an email, and send it off to your favorite folks. Don't forget to add a catchy subject line, like "Prepare to Be Amazed by My Toy-tacular Video!"

2. Social Media Magic: If your parents allow you to use social media, sharing your video there can be a fantastic way to reach your friends and family. Whether it's Facebook, Instagram, Twitter, or another platform, just hit the "share" button, add a snazzy caption, and let the likes and comments roll in.

3. The WhatsApp Whiz: With the blessing of your parents, send your video link through WhatsApp or other messaging apps to your friends and family. Just tap the paperclip icon, select the link to your video, and add a message like, "Check out my latest toy adventure!"

4. YouTube's Built-In Sharing: Did you know that YouTube has its own sharing feature? Just click the "Share" button under your video, and you can send it directly to your friends on YouTube. You can even create a playlist of your videos to share!

5. Show and Tell: For a more personal touch, invite your friends over for a viewing party. Grab some popcorn, gather around the TV or computer, and let the toy adventures begin! There's nothing like watching your video with an audience and hearing their laughter and applause.

Sharing your videos with friends and family is like sprinkling extra sparkles on an already magical experience. As your loved ones watch your toy-tastic creation, they'll be reminded of your creativity, humor, and the joy that only a good toy story can bring. So go forth, young YouTuber, and share your video with pride – you've earned your spot in the toy video hall of fame!

the social media superhero's guide to promoting videos responsibly

Great googly moogly, you've done it! You've created an amazing toy video, and now you want to share it with the world. But hold your horses, young YouTuber! It's important to be a responsible social media superhero when promoting your videos. So grab your cape, and let's dive into the world of responsible social media sharing.

1. Get Parental Permission: First things first – always check with your parents before posting anything online. They're your trusty sidekicks in this digital world, and they'll help you make sure your online activities are safe and sound.
2. Keep It Private: When sharing your videos on social media, remember to adjust your privacy settings so that only your friends and family can see them. This way, you're sharing your toy-tastic creations with the people who matter most, while also keeping your content safe from any internet supervillains.
3. Be Kind and Positive: Just like superheroes fight for justice, use your social media powers for good! Share positive messages, and be kind and respectful to everyone who comments on your videos. Remember, with great power comes great responsibility!
4. Don't Overdo It: You might be excited to share your video with the world, but try not to spam your friends with too many posts. Limit yourself to one or two posts per video to keep things fun and fresh for your audience.

5. The Golden Rule: Treat others as you'd like to be treated. Before sharing your video, ask yourself, "Would I want someone to share this with me?" If the answer is yes, then you're on the right track.
6. Know When to Unplug: While it's fun to share your videos and see the reactions from your friends, it's also essential to take breaks from screens and social media. Make sure to enjoy other activities and spend quality time with family and friends in the real world too.

By following these guidelines, you'll not only be a YouTube star but also a social media superhero, using your powers responsibly to spread joy and laughter through your toy videos. And remember, young YouTuber, with a cape, a smile, and a dash of responsibility, you can conquer the world – one toy video at a time!

the fantabulous fusion of youtuber friendships

Calling all young YouTubers, it's time for a YouTube party! Imagine teaming up with your fellow toy video creators to form a super-duper, fantabulous fusion of YouTuber friendships. This is where the magic of collaboration and cross-promotion comes in. So, buckle up and get ready for a wild ride of teamwork and fun!

1. Find Your YouTube BFFs: Start by searching for other young YouTubers who make videos like yours. Look for creators with a similar audience, style, and sense of humor. You can find them by searching on YouTube or joining online forums and groups for young creators.
2. Reach Out and Say "Howdy!": Once you've found your potential YouTube BFFs, reach out to them with a friendly message. Tell them how much you admire their work and ask if they'd like to collaborate on a video together. Remember, everyone loves a nice compliment!
3. Brainstorm Together: Get your creative juices flowing by brainstorming video ideas with your new YouTube pals. You could create a toy battle, a toy fashion show, or even a toy cooking competition! The sky's the limit when you put your imaginative minds together.

4. Share the Spotlight: When you create a collaborative video, make sure everyone gets their moment to shine. Feature each other's toys, take turns speaking, and celebrate each other's unique talents. It's like a YouTube talent show, and everyone's a winner!
5. Cross-Promote Like a Boss: After you've created your epic collaboration, it's time to share it with the world. Post the video on each of your channels and give a shout-out to your fellow collaborators. Encourage your viewers to check out your new YouTube friends' channels, and watch your fan bases grow together.
6. Keep the Party Going: Just like with any good friendship, it's essential to stay in touch with your YouTube BFFs. Keep supporting each other's work, and don't be afraid to collaborate on more fantastic videos in the future.

So, young YouTubers, it's time to unite, collaborate, and let your toy-loving friendships soar to new heights. By joining forces with other amazing creators, you'll not only have a blast, but you'll also make the world of YouTube an even more fun and fabulous place to be!

9 /
staying safe online: a guide for kids and parents

the super-duper guide to staying safe on youtube!

AHOY, young YouTubers! Ready to explore the wild, wacky, and sometimes slippery world of online safety? Well, strap on your safety helmets and hold on to your favorite stuffed animals, because we're going on a YouTube safety adventure!

1. Secret Identity, Assemble!: Just like superheroes, you need to keep your real identity under wraps. Don't share personal details like your full name, address, or school. Stick to your cool YouTube alias, like "Captain ToyMaster5000"!

2. Buddy System, Activate!: When browsing YouTube, always use the buddy system. That means watching videos with your parents or another trusted grown-up nearby. They're like your trusty sidekicks, ready to help you out of any sticky situation!
3. The Power of the Pause Button: Remember, you control the video! If something feels weird or makes you uncomfortable, hit that pause button like a superhero saving the day. Then, tell a grown-up about it so they can help you figure out what to do next.
4. Comment Commandments: When leaving comments, be as kind and friendly as a fluffy bunny. Remember, there's a real person behind every video, and they have feelings too. If someone leaves you a not-so-nice comment, don't be a copycat – just ignore it and tell a grown-up.
5. Password Power-Up: Keep your YouTube password a top-secret mystery, like the location of the lost city of Atlantis. Don't share it with anyone, except your parents or guardians. The more mysterious your password, the safer your channel will be!

So, there you have it, fellow YouTube adventurers! By following these super-duper safety tips, you'll be able to explore the exciting world of YouTube while staying safe and sound. With great power (and awesome toy videos) comes great responsibility!

parental powers: unlocking the secrets of online safety!

Calling all super-parents! Are you ready to embark on a thrilling mission to ensure your child's safety while they explore the vast online universe? Great! Let's dive into the top-secret tactics that will turn you into the ultimate online safety guardians.

1. Sneaky Supervision: Keep an eye on your child's online activities, but do it with the stealth of a ninja. Be present, but not too overbearing. Encourage open communication and let them know they can share anything with you, even if it's a video of a cat playing the piano.
2. The Great Firewall: Employ the powers of parental controls to create a virtual fortress around your child's internet use. Set up filters, time limits, and monitor their online

adventures to ensure they're not wandering into unknown territories.

3. Top-Secret Training: Educate your little online explorers about the importance of privacy, and how to recognize and report suspicious behavior. Make it fun by creating a family game night around online safety trivia – winner gets extra dessert!

4. Gadget Ground Rules: Establish a set of family rules for using gadgets, like keeping devices in shared spaces or setting screen-time limits. Make sure you follow the rules too, because parents can set an example even while battling alien invaders in a video game.

5. Cyber-Squad: Connect with other parents to create a network of online safety superheroes. Share your wisdom, learn from others, and join forces to protect your kids from the dark side of the internet.

By following these secret strategies, you'll become the ultimate protectors of your child's online world. With your newfound parental powers, you can ensure a safe and fun digital experience for your little ones. Together, you'll conquer the internet like the super-family you are!

the art of dodging cyber-baddies and their mean messages

Hey, awesome kids! Sometimes, while we're having a blast sharing our toy videos with the world, a few cyber-baddies might sneak in and leave not-so-nice comments. Fear not, because we've got the ultimate guide to dodge those mean messages and stand up to cyberbullies like a superhero!

1. Build a Cyber-Fortress: First things first – make your online space as safe as possible. Set your privacy settings to the max and only accept friend requests from people you know. Think of it like building an epic pillow fort that only your best buddies can enter!
2. Don't Feed the Trolls: If you spot a negative comment or message, remember the golden rule – don't feed the trolls! They're hungry for attention, but if you ignore them, they'll eventually slink back into the dark corners of the internet.
3. The Super-Blocker Move: If someone's being a real cyber-baddie, unleash your inner superhero and use the power of the

block button. With one click, you can make the baddies disappear, like magic!

4. Call in the Reinforcements: If cyberbullying gets too tough to handle, don't be afraid to ask for help. Tell your parents, teachers, or other trusted adults. They'll swoop in like a team of superheroes to save the day!

5. Spread Positivity: Lastly, be the hero you are by spreading positivity and kindness online. Leave encouraging comments, support your friends, and create a positive online atmosphere. Remember, superheroes always fight for what's right!

Now you're ready to dodge those cyber-baddies and their mean messages like a pro. Keep your online world a happy and safe place, and don't let anyone steal your superhero shine!

becoming a pretend play toy video star: tips for success

the secret sauce of superstar channels: consistency and creativity!

Gather 'round, young video masters, and listen closely as we reveal the two magical ingredients that can transform your YouTube channel from ho-hum to HOLY COW! These not-so-secret ingredients are consistency and creativity. Let's mix up a batch of YouTube success!

1. The Tick-Tock of Consistency: Just like how your favorite superhero arrives right on time to save the day, you should aim to post your videos regularly. This could be once a week, every other day, or whatever works for you. Your fans will appreciate

knowing when to expect your next awesome toy video!
2. The Ever-Changing Creative Cape: Superheroes need to change up their strategies to outwit villains, and so do you! Keep your channel fresh and exciting by trying new video ideas, toy scenarios, or filming styles. Your fans will be on the edge of their seats, waiting for your next creative masterpiece!
3. Calendar of Greatness: To help you stay on track with your super-consistency, create a video calendar. Plan your videos in advance, so you're always ready to swoop in and save the day with a brand new video!
4. Creative Brainstorming Sessions: When you're feeling stuck in a creativity rut, grab your trusty sidekick (a friend or family member) and brainstorm new video ideas together. Two superhero minds are better than one!
5. Learn from the YouTube Legends: Watch other popular YouTubers for inspiration. Learn from their successes (and their mistakes) to help you level up your own

channel. But remember, always be true to your unique super-self!

By mastering the magical mix of consistency and creativity, your channel will grow faster than a speeding bullet! Keep your fans entertained, and your channel will soar to new heights, just like your favorite superhero!

soaring high and staying grounded: a guide to fame for the young youtuber

Listen up, future YouTube stars! As you rocket toward fame and glory, it's important to remember that with great power comes great responsibility. To help you stay grounded while you soar, we've put together a few tips to keep you humble, kind, and ready to face the world!

1. The Super Squad: Surround yourself with friends and family who've been there since the beginning. These trusty sidekicks will remind you of your roots and keep your head from floating away into the clouds.
2. Superhero School: Just like how even superheroes need to learn and practice, continue to work on your craft. Always

strive to improve your video-making skills, learn from others, and never think you're too cool for school.

3. The Gratitude Goggles: Don't forget to appreciate your fans and supporters! They're the ones who've helped you achieve your dreams, so be sure to thank them for their love and encouragement.
4. The Kindness Cape: As your channel grows, so does your influence. Use your newfound fame for good by being kind, respectful, and considerate in your interactions with others, both online and offline.
5. The Humble Hat: Remember, fame can be fleeting. Don't let it go to your head or define your self-worth. Stay true to yourself and appreciate the journey, not just the destination.

In the end, it's essential to stay grounded as your YouTube channel takes off. By keeping these tips in mind, you'll be able to handle fame with grace and poise, just like the superhero you are! Your fans will love you even more for being a genuinely awesome person – both on and off the screen.

soaring high and staying grounded: a guide to fame for the young youtuber

Listen up, future YouTube stars! As you rocket toward fame and glory, it's important to remember that with great power comes great responsibility. To help you stay grounded while you soar, we've put together a few tips to keep you humble, kind, and ready to face the world!

1. The Super Squad: Surround yourself with friends and family who've been there since the beginning. These trusty sidekicks will remind you of your roots and keep your head from floating away into the clouds.
2. Superhero School: Just like how even superheroes need to learn and practice, continue to work on your craft. Always strive to improve your video-making skills, learn from others, and never think you're too cool for school.
3. The Gratitude Goggles: Don't forget to appreciate your fans and supporters! They're the ones who've helped you achieve your dreams, so be sure to thank them for their love and encouragement.

4. The Kindness Cape: As your channel grows, so does your influence. Use your newfound fame for good by being kind, respectful, and considerate in your interactions with others, both online and offline.
5. The Humble Hat: Remember, fame can be fleeting. Don't let it go to your head or define your self-worth. Stay true to yourself and appreciate the journey, not just the destination.

In the end, it's essential to stay grounded as your YouTube channel takes off. By keeping these tips in mind, you'll be able to handle fame with grace and poise, just like the superhero you are! Your fans will love you even more for being a genuinely awesome person – both on and off the screen.

conclusion: the adventure continues

the cake and oops! chronicles: successes and slip-ups

Gather 'round, young YouTubers, as we embark on a wild adventure through the land of achievements and the jungle of mistakes. Spoiler alert: it's a thrilling ride!

1. Cake Chronicles: Let's start with the scrumptious stuff – your achievements! When you reach a milestone, like your first 100 subscribers or a well-edited video, it's time to celebrate! Throw yourself a mini party, dance like no one's watching, or devour a slice of cake (or two)!

2. Bravo, Buddy: Share your successes with friends, family, and your YouTube community. They've been cheering you on from the start, so let them join in the celebrations. Who knows, they might even bring more cake!
3. Oops! Jungle: Now, let's explore the wild world of mistakes. Guess what? Everyone makes them! It's part of being human. Your YouTube journey will have its share of slip-ups, but don't worry – they're just learning opportunities in disguise.
4. The Bounce-Back: When you stumble, dust yourself off, and get back up. Analyze what went wrong and how you can improve. Turn that "oops" into an "aha!" moment that will make you an even better content creator.
5. Humor Hack: Laugh it off! If you can find the humor in your mistakes, you'll be able to keep your spirits high and your audience entertained. Plus, laughter is the best medicine (well, besides cake).

In the wild world of YouTube, you'll experience both the Cake Chronicles and the Oops! Jungle. Celebrate your achievements, learn from your mistakes, and you'll come out on the other side as a fearless, fun-loving content creator. So grab your explorer hat, and let's get ready to conquer the Cake and Oops! Chronicles together!

toytube time-travel: a peek into the future

Fasten your seatbelts, young YouTubers, as we blast off into the future of pretend play toy videos and YouTube! (No need for a time machine—we've got your imagination!)

1. New Toys, New Adventures: As toy makers keep inventing new, out-of-this-world toys, the possibilities for your videos will skyrocket! Get ready to explore the far reaches of the galaxy, dive into the depths of the ocean, or discover magical realms with your trusty toys.
2. Tech-Tastic: The future of YouTube will be filled with even more fantastic technology. Prepare for mind-blowing virtual reality experiences, holographic toy adventures, and other high-tech wonders that'll make your videos extra-special.

Conclusion: The Adventure Continues

3. Global Toy Party: As YouTube continues to connect people from all around the world, your pretend play toy videos will reach even more viewers. This means more friends, more fun, and the chance to learn about different toys and cultures. Hooray for international toy parties!
4. YouTube Evolution: Like all things in life, YouTube will keep evolving. There might be new features, rules, and ways to engage with your audience. Stay on your toes, young content creators, and be ready to adapt and grow with the platform.
5. The Power of Play: No matter what changes come to YouTube or the toy world, one thing will always remain the same: the power of imagination and play. Your creativity, passion, and love for pretend play will continue to shine through in your videos, capturing the hearts of viewers everywhere.

So, as we teleport back to the present, remember that the future is a wild, wacky, and wonderful place full of exciting possibilities for pretend play toy videos and YouTube. Keep dreaming, keep playing, and keep creating, young YouTubers, because the future is yours to shape!

toy videos: your ticket to a world of possibilities

Hold on to your hats, kids, because we're about to reveal how making toy videos can lead you to amazing future careers and passions! It's like finding a golden ticket inside a chocolate bar, but better!

1. Future Film Directors: Creating toy videos helps you master the art of storytelling and learn the ins and outs of filmmaking. Who knows? One day, you might be yelling "Action!" on the set of your very own blockbuster movie!
2. Animation Nation: Love adding animations and special effects to your videos? You might have a bright future as an animator, breathing life into your own cartoon characters or working for a famous animation studio. High five, future Pixar pals!
3. Toy Design Tycoon: If you've got a knack for dreaming up new toy adventures, you

Conclusion: The Adventure Continues

could become a toy designer! Invent the next big plaything and watch as kids around the world have a blast with your creations.

4. Acting Up a Storm: Channeling your inner thespian as you voice your toy characters? You might just find your calling as an actor or voiceover artist, shining in the spotlight on stage, screen, or behind the microphone.
5. Tech Whiz Kids: All that video editing, audio tweaking, and technical know-how could lead to a career in the tech industry. You'll be the one inventing new gadgets, apps, or even the next YouTube!
6. Mini Marketing Masterminds: Promoting your videos, managing your channel, and growing your audience are great skills to have. You could become a marketing guru or social media wizard, helping businesses reach new heights.

As you can see, creating toy videos is like opening a treasure chest full of exciting future paths. It's not just about having fun now (although that's important too!), but it's also about discovering your passions and unlocking your potential. Keep on playing, experimenting, and learning, young YouTubers, because you never know where your toy videos might take you!